Maria Marsh was born in Finland in 1987. As the second oldest and the only girl, she struggled to find her place in the world. She married her first husband when she was only 19; it lasted over 10 years, giving the couple a daughter, Joanna, in 2010. In 2013 her husband was diagnosed with colon cancer, and within a year it was terminal. Three-and-a-half years later he succumbed to his illness, leaving behind a 6-year-old daughter and a 29-year-old widow. She found her strength to go on in her daughter and in writing. Although she had been writing various stories since her teenage years, she now had a story that needed sharing, a story that wouldn't stay in her cupboard. A real story, of love, of hardship, of forgiveness, the story of her life she never saw coming. Maria moved with her daughter to all the way to England to start over. She remarried in 2018 and is now happy fulfilling her lifelong dream of writing full time.

I would like to dedicate this book to my family: my superhero dad, who stood by me through the toughest times in our lives; to my husband, for his unending support and love. And to my friends, who didn't abandon me when I needed them the most.

Maria Marsh

I Miss You, I Love You, I Hate You

A wife's journey in the shadow of her husband's terminal cancer

Austin Macauley Publishers™
London • Cambridge • New York • Sharjah

All of the events in this memoir are true to the best of author's memory. The views expressed in this memoir are solely those of the author.

A CIP catalogue record for this title is available from the British Library.

ISBN 9781528982481 (Paperback)
ISBN 9781528982498 (ePub e-book)

www.austinmacauley.com

First Published (2021)
Austin Macauley Publishers Ltd
25 Canada Square
Canary Wharf
London
E14 5LQ

I would like to thank Austin Macauley Publishers for believing in me and my story, for helping me through the process of publication and for making my dream come true. I would like to thank every person involved in getting my story out there.

Chapter 1

I started writing when I was just a kid. I didn't know at the time, that it would take another fifteen years, before I found something worthy to write about, something I needed to write about. I've started to write about so many different things over the years, never truly satisfied with the content, not knowing, that there would be a story, just not the kind I ever imagined.

There are so many blogs, so many inspirational videos, so many good books about cancer, mostly from cancer survivals or those that are still battling it. That's how mine started, as a blog, something where I could truly honestly in its raw most emotional form, write about what my family was going through, what I was going through.

But I noticed something. There wasn't many blogs or books about those that lived in the shadow of those that were sick or dying. I found a few, but not many. So that's my reason for writing this book, to give a voice to those that feel forgotten, to help validate their feelings too. To make sure that my story doesn't stay unheard. This is the reality, this was my reality.

I'm not trying to dismiss the people that have cancer, that their feelings are somehow invalid in all this, they most certainly are not. My story however, is my story, our story, what it was really like to live with a terminal diagnosis, what we went through every single day, how it impacted us, as individuals and as a family.

This book for me, it's painful, it's beyond hard, it's healing and it has taught me so much along the way. My hope is, that the person reading this, can find a little piece of healing too, that you can say, I'm allowed to feel too, I'm allowed to fall down too, that I have a voice too! It's not selfish, it's healthy.

There are so many things I didn't know back then, and I didn't know how to voice my opinion and my feelings, how to be heard, truly heard, I didn't know how to ask for help. I'm here to inspire others to be braver than what I was.

Chapter 2

I started my blog, called, cancer and every day – cancer sucks but life doesn't, in July 2016, just five months before my husband passed away from terminal colon cancer. I have to say, I don't think I believed even then that he was dying. All in all, he fought this illness for three and a half years, he was 37 when he died. I was a 29-year-old widow, with a small child, utterly lost.

My man, he was the most stubborn man I ever knew, which is why it took his workplace by surprise when I called them to inform them of his passing, since he only went on sick leave two months earlier.

This was my first blog post:

Day like any other July 19th 2016

'By now, it's been about three years since my husband got diagnosed ..and life has definitely changed..

At first you couldn't even tell that he was sick ..then became the surgeries and radiation etc ..and then the not so magical day when we were told that nothing more can be done, that now it was about the quality of life, and maybe prolonging the inevitable by drugs ..yeah ..not what you or anyone wants to hear ..EVER.

I was at work when the call came, he sounded so calm, it was weird, I don't think it had sunk in yet for him. It was a short call, I guess in the end he was trying to keep himself together. My reaction to it, was to walk out to the smoking area, even though I had stopped smoking years before, and cry my bloody eyes out.

But even on that day ..you couldn't really tell that he was sick ..not yet ..there was no pain or really any symptoms, not the worrying kind anyway..

He did have symptoms, he just never shared them with me, not until it was too late, another learned behavior from his family. We started with radiation after surgery, but it made him so ill, and none of the anti-nausea meds helped. So we had to have a serious talk, talk about the quality of life.

So we decided to stop taking any more radiation or any other drugs to that related, and for over a year went by ..and nothing, he was feeling good, no symptoms, no pain ..nothing ..I guess looking back at that time now, you realize that you've taken that time for granted, you didn't even realize that those days ..they were a blessing..

The doctors told us, if we decided to stop taking preventative measures, a.k.a. the radiation and the lot, that the cancer would spread, because it was an aggressive kind of cancer, and that he wouldn't live to see the year end. How wrong they were.. So at this point, one year after his initial diagnosis, we had had the terminal diagnosis, and decided to live our lives as best we knew, without medications that made his live an utter misery.

Than the day came, when things turned around ..he was in pain ..he was bleeding ..his hemoglobin was at an all-time low ..deadly low..

It's been about surviving each day ever since ..getting up in the morning ..He has had to increase his pain meds a lot since those first days ..he can't go without them ..and it's scary ..really scary..

I don't think either of us realized, what our reality was going to change into, from living a normal life, to taking pain medicine that costs almost 1000 euros at the time, thank god we didn't have to pay for it, but every time we go out to buy some more, the actual price is in the package, and it's mind blowing.

It's kills something inside you ..watching the man you love just wither away in front of you ..to see him getting weaker, to see him depressed ..there have been nights when I couldn't sleep at all, and I would just lie next to him, listening to him breathe..'

I've read through my blog a few times, in all honesty, it probably took me months before I could start reading through them, it hurt too much, because I can see the emotions shining through every word, and it still hurts, but now it's like a dull pain in my heart, instead of a silent scream inside me. Some things still make me shake my head, like the cost of pain relieve for cancer patients, even though our government or whatever is paying them, after you've reached a certain limit, as in used enough money yourself first. It's absolutely ridiculous. The only people that were truly helpful to us in the end, was the hospice people. They treated us like normal people, not like sick people. Don't get me wrong, they had the knowledge and all about how to look after my husband medically, but they treated us like family, like we were normal. Most people we met over the years, had that pitying look in their eyes, always saying “I’m so sorry” and as much as we could appreciate that, it did get annoying at times. We didn’t want to be known only for the fact that my husband had terminal cancer, it was actually nice to talk about anything else but that with people.

Here’s my next one, which pretty much speaks for itself.

Don’t you just Hate it! July 19th 2016

‘OMG! I ..no let me rephrase that ..we hate it, when people come to us saying; well maybe it’s God’s will that you have cancer, that He has a bigger plan for us ..that God wants another angel in heaven ..that it’s simply God saying, you’re time is up.. WHAT!?!

What is wrong with you people!?

It’s not God’s plan or timing or whatever that people have cancer, it’s not His will. He is not an evil God, I refuse to believe that.

I get so mad when I hear this ..but than you realize something ..we are all broken people in a broken world, and we desperately need the comfort that these phrases bring us ..but the fact remains ..you shouldn’t say something like that to a person with cancer, those phrases are for the people left behind, after losing someone, for them, it brings comfort, hope, some closure..’

The second post says it all. The last months, were so hard, emotionally, physically, mentally, you name it. I was so angry, so frustrated. I felt like screaming. Looking back now,

I understand people better, and I understand me better. Lot of times, people sincerely don't know what to say, so they either say nothing, which I applaud, or they say something really stupid. Just to let you know, a lot of times, those of us going through hard times, we don't need you to say anything, we need you to be there, just be there, and wait for us to ask, or better yet, ask what you can do, because like I said before, I didn't know how to ask, so please people, ask your friends, ask your loved ones, your family, what do they really need.

Here's one tip that was a lifesaver for me: my best friend at the time, told me, that when things get so bad, when you feel like screaming, just call me and I will drive us somewhere less populated area, and you can scream you're head off. Let me tell you people, it really helps. Instead of screaming to your loved ones, or bawling your eyes out at work, or heaven forbid, throw plates and what not to the walls, get a trusted friend, go out, and literally let it all out.

Here's my next entry:

The good and the bad July 19th 2016

'There is always going to be good days and bad days, sometimes, the good and the bad are in the same day ..what you do with it, I think is the key.

Do you stay locked inside your home, feeling sorry for yourself, or do you choose a different attitude. Easier said than done right..?

You have no idea how many times I and we have just remained home feeling sorry for ourselves ..I guess that's part of it all ..You just have to choose ..no matter what your day is like..

Choose to be happy, for the little moments of laughter, those smiles, little things, that all of a sudden seem huge.

You really start to appreciate life more, when you're face to face with death..

There are days that just suck ..when you're head feels like it's going to blow ..but you learn to take it one thing, one day at a time..

Right now we are wondering if my husband can go back to work at all, after his holidays end ..nothing's been decided yet ..we're just talking...yeah ..except this talk has been going on for months on end ..I hate the insecurity that this situation makes me feel.

There's always these really crappy days ..when my husband is at his lowest ..and all he does is sleep and cry, and say that he wants to die rather than feel sick all day everyday ..but then he picks up the pieces again ..and goes back to work like any normal person ..until that bad day hits again ..and let me tell you those bad days seem to come more often than not these days

Yeah, I know what you're going to say ..duh ..he has terminal cancer ..of course he's mad, and sad and depressed..

I know ..but everything that he does or doesn't do, everything that he goes through, all of it ..it affects this entire family, not just him ..yeah ..I'm selfish right for saying that, I mean he is the one dying ..not me ..right..

What some people don't get, is that when a person get's cancer, his or her entire family get's cancer..'

It kills me to read this, it raises so many different emotions in me, and yet going through this, from the beginning, let's me see it in a very different perspective. It also shows many important things I want to raise to your attention. The one very important fact, is that cancer indeed affects more than that one person who is actually sick, the entire family suffers alongside them. I do admit, there was a lot of anger inside me during that time. I felt like my husband was shutting me out, emotionally and physically. He didn't want to know what was going on, he was in denial to the very day he passed away. It's hard to watch. The person you've known for over a decade, you've been married to this guy for ten years, and now, you don't even know this person anymore. I don't blame him, I used to, I used to hate him, but I see now, that that was his way of dealing with it, right or wrong, he had a right to his emotions too. But so did I, and that's my inspiration for this book, to finally be heard, from my perspective.

Taking it one moment, one day or one week at a time, is a good idea, however, it doesn't always work. You may tell yourself that it does, but it's really hard not to let everything fall on top of you and drowning you with it. You need to take a breather, whether you want to or not. Go out for a walk, get a coffee, see a movie, get your head out of the situation, or you will lose your mind.

My way was working, too much, which just added to the existing stress. I didn't go out, not by myself, and not with friends, I felt too guilty to go. I was slowly but surely going mad, but my rescue was my blog, I got to really vent my feelings, even though I knew that sometimes what I said, was not received well, and it made people mad. Go figure. Although I did notice that people received fairly well my blog posts while he was still alive, they felt sorry for me and mine, and were more lenient with my posts, but the second he was gone, every single step I took, was scrutinized and criticized. In the end I had to stop writing anything anymore in that blog, because the way it was received was mind blowing too, and I even started getting phone calls, from people I now refer as friends that are no longer my friends.

It got bad, everybody had an opinion about how I should grieve and how long and everything else. I got nasty phone calls and messages, saying how I should take things off from Facebook, since I put my blog there too, I got messages that said that they were disappointed in me, and that I should be home bawling my eyes out, I should show everyone around me how crushed I am. Needless to say, a lot of the feedback I got, made me really sad, and I lost a lot of so called friends along the way.

I know that to some, I won't say most, but to some, these self-help books are a life saver, books that have certain steps. I know there's books about the steps of grieve, there's books about accepting a terminal diagnosis and many more. There's one thing they have in common, they have different stages that you go through. For me, I hated those books, I've always thought that it's not important what someone else says you should be doing, but what does your heart, mind and body tell you. There's no right way to grieve, only your way. In the end, people don't know you, well not everyone, and you need to be aware of that, you need to stand firm and say, this is how I'm handling things, if you don't like it, the screw it. Keep the right people in your life, not the negative ones, the ones who always think they are right no matter what.

I was hurting, I was grieving, even though some people in my life said, I wasn't. I was married for over ten years. He was my best friend, my support, my everything. I hated seeing him sick, I hated how it changed him, I hated the fact that he left us. But I had a daughter to think about, I had to show her, that in the midst of all that grief and sorrow, that life had to move on. I was 29 for god's sake, I had my whole life ahead of me. I thought for a brief second that I wouldn't ever be with someone else, but I'm glad I was wrong.

No one can tell you how to live your life, no one can tell you how to grieve, no one can tell you time lines for anything. I don't believe, for a second, that my husband wanted me to stay alone for the rest of my life. I do understand that there are people in the world who think that they only get one soul mate, and if they lose that, they will never find another, and that's fine by me. I personally, don't think we're meant to be alone, you can find love and peace all over, if you only take a chance, and that does mean, that you open your heart again, even when it hurts.

Chapter 3

I want to talk more about using our voices, to be heard, let me first put my blog post here.

I'm here too July 20th 2016

'During the first year ..I noticed something weird (to me at least) people kept coming to us, coming to me and asking, how's my husband doing, how's he coping etc, but not once did they ask, how was the rest of the family..

Maybe it was still the initial shock of it all, I know that we were still trying to wrap our heads around the news of having cancer, but still..

It wasn't until later, that people started asking how's the family ..but to be honest, that first year, that was the hardest time ever for our family, so on that note, that would have been the best time to have more support ..but than again, at that time, I didn't really know how and what to ask of people around us..

I guess it's no ones fault ..it's just something that's been on my mind. Hopefully we all can learn from these experiences..'

It speaks volumes, why? Why weren't we important enough for people to ask how we were? Is it an honest mistake? Did they mean us, when they asked how he was doing? It made me pretty angry. I was there every single day, did my wellbeing mean less then him? It's not about refocusing people's attentions from a sick person to me, but realizing that cancer affects us all. It's like I stopped living for all those years when he was sick and to the day when he passed and beyond. I lived for him, my sole focus was him, his sickness, his treatments, his surgeries, his moods. I didn't exist anymore, I lost my voice.

There should be more information about these situations, and more available to the public, one more reason to write this book. I had no idea, where to go to, to get help, to find a professional to talk to. We only found that help in the last five months once we entered the hospice. They had therapist for everything, including a child therapist that was so needed for my little girl. She needed someone to talk to, she needed to be spoken very plainly about the upcoming events, including her dad's death. I had no idea how to approach that subject, but the therapist made it so effortless, in the midst of playing with my daughter, they were able to talk about even death, and I have to say, that even though I had been avoiding that conversion, I was now very relieved that that subject was out. My daughter needed all the time she got, to get used to or adjust to that idea. I don't think you can ever get used to it, you just learn to live with it.

It's been over two years now, since he died, I've moved to another country with my little girl, who is now 9, I'm remarried, I'm finding my own voice again, finding who I am without the shadow of death upon me. I'm happy. But in order to heal completely and learn from my past mistakes, I'm rehashing the past, the good the bad and the ugly, in the hopes, that what I went through, and what I've learned over the years, will someday help someone else, facing the similar situation. I know it feels like a giant in front of you, but you will overcome, I did.

Let's go back to my next entry:

Real men don't cry July 20th 2016

'I call it as I see it, and it's bullshit! Real men do cry, real men are able to talk about they're feelings ..but it doesn't mean it's easy..

But you know after a decade of being together, you don't really need to talk ..you know without words how the other persons feeling..

Until my hubby got sick, I hadn't seen him cry, more than twice, in the entire time we've been together ..but nowadays ..he cries more than I do ..He cries in the car a lot, at home, while visiting family and friends ..I guess that says a lot about his state of mind these days..

So what though ..A real man show's his emotions, and I'm so proud of my husband!'

I was thinking about this as I read through it again, and I realized, that it's something I had forgotten. See the first year after he was gone, was bad, I was so lost without him, and I was angry, angry that he fought for so long and then he just gave up, I was angry because he left me, and the only memories at that point, were all about his last months, especially his last week that we spent in hospice. For some reason I couldn't remember all those good years we had together, I was too distraught, too angry, too lost in my own grief. But slowly as time has gone forward, I've started to remember more and more of those beautiful memories we did make together.

I didn't even realize that being angry at someone who has died, was a normal part of grieving, and at first I was so ashamed of my feelings, before I realized that it's something that grieving people go through, that feeling and so much more.

It is so important, that, especially in a relationship, you have to let the other person in, in order for your relationship to work. But in all honesty, it's easier said than done. Until you find yourself in a situation like this, where you're battling to come to terms with a terminal diagnosis, you just don't know how you'll react, you think you do, but trust me, you don't. That's ok though, if my years with my first husband taught me anything, it's to show mercy to your spouse and to yourself. There's no right way to react to news like that. There's only your way.

Be honest, be straightforward, but be kind, don't be cruel, and if you mess it up, say something you regret later, forgive yourself and others, and let it go, you're only human.

You do go through so many different emotions over time as you're grieving, sometimes it's one particular feeling on a particular day, sometimes its five different emotions. Give yourself time, listen to what your heart is telling you, not what other people are telling you.

I was told that I should've grieved my husband at least two years, that I had no right to start dating any sooner, but then there were other friends that said to me, I'm so glad you've found love again, I was so worried that you never would, knowing how important you're first husband was to you, but I'm proud of you, for letting a new person in. Now that is what I meant, when I said before, to have only positive people in your life. Your true friends, will always support you, even if they don't understand your decisions.

There's one thing you do have to remember though. People react differently to grief, that includes you too, and sometimes that grief makes us say things we regret later. It may mean, that you need to put some time and distance between some people in your life, but don't shut the door completely, you might regret that later on. I know I did that, I was still grieving, and the last thing I needed was bullshit from people that I called friends and family, and I haven't spoken to some of them since, because words can wound, but so can pride.

Chapter 4

What now? July 26th 2016

'You know when we got diagnosed, the first question is, was, what now, what happens now, what are we going to do, how long do we have.. I know I keep saying us and we, coz cancer always affects the entire family, we have cancer, we are dealing with it, we are fighting it, TOGETHER!

Just because you were declared terminal, doesn't mean you stop fighting, doesn't mean you stop believing, and hoping, and just living.

When we found out that he was terminal ..my first reaction was, ok, we need to put up a list, you know a bucket-list, what are the things that he wants to do before ..you know...before he dies ..The list never happened ..why ..because here is what my husband said to me;

I want to grow old with, I want to have more babies with you, I want to see our grandchildren and he didn't say it like all sad, knowing that he would never get to do that, but he said it, with hope, with confidence, with determination to live ..That's my husband!

All though our reality is very different from what we thought it would be, since we never thought he would get

cancer, at age 34, it's just part of our lives, it doesn't change who we are, or what our hopes for the future are.

I'm not saying it's easy, coz it's not, there are really bad days, and then there are ok days, some good days, and some great. But you just have to take one hour at a time, one day, one week at a time. What you need to remember is that those really bad moment's, they don't define who you are ..you're going to hit rock bottom, and then you climb back up.'

Oh god, reading this brings back memories. I wrote this one, on a good day, when we were both feeling better, I so took for granted those few good days we had, and it kills me to admit that, but I did, we did. You see, to us, those days still went in a fog, it was hard to be grateful, for the little moments we had that were good.

I wrote about how you don't stop believing and hoping and just living, but we did, how did I not see that before. We put up this front in front of the world, our friends, our family, to make it seem like we were alright, but we weren't. We were smiling on the outside, but crying and screaming on the inside. We felt like we were cheated, like the whole universe was against us. This wasn't our plan, this isn't how we wanted to live our lives. But reality for us, really sucked.

We didn't know, how much time we had left, no one did.

When you just want more time July 27th 2016

'So this is how it feels, when the whole world holds its breath ..When you feel like time just stopped moving, for a split second, everything stops ..

We were just told that most likely, we only have a few months left, which was a shock...I mean we knew, that most

likely time was not on our side, but to be told, that he might not make it through this year ..was a shock ..that he might not be here this Christmas ..

What am I supposed to say to that, how am I supposed to feel ..other than numb ..Completely numb.

I want more time, we want more time.

It's so hard to wrap your head around this matter ..which may sound weird, coz we've had this terminal diagnosis for so long now, that it's just simply become a part of our everyday life, and yet the idea of him actually dying ..is incomprehensible

And yet again, I'm not willing to cast out all hope, and just stop fighting, I don't want to fall apart, coz I'm not sure how I'm going to get up again. If ever there was a time, when I need to be strong, for my family, that's now.

A positive attitude can change worlds. I need to believe that.

Although we still have hope for tomorrow, at the same time, my mind runs around thinking, how am I suppose to prepare for this, how can I prepare my child for this, what are the things I need to do now..

I wish I had all the answers, I wish I could see the future..'

I don't know if seeing into the future, would've helped. I wrote this particular blog post in the end of July, and we didn't know that, by Christmas, he would indeed be gone. It twists my heart to think about all the things that happened just in the last five months of his life.

The doctors didn't know, and they weren't really allowed to give any specific time lines, the first time they did, they said that if he stopped his medications, chemo and such, he wouldn't live beyond the first year, when in fact he fought the cancer for nearly four years. The next time, the doctors said that his health was deteriorating so fast, that they gave him only a few months, he lasted five. A week before Christmas, he passed away.

He fought like a true warrior, for our sake for his family, but when he decided that he'd had enough, that he was too tired to fight, his body just stopped fighting and he went pretty fast after that.

I got my first tattoo after his passing, just the word warrior, because that's what he was to me, and furthermore, that's what I was and my daughter. Warriors. I thought we would crumble underneath the weight of it all, but we're here today, doing pretty good, so I'd say we deserve to be called warriors.

We did want more time, we wanted all the time in the world, but we lived a lifetime in the ten years we did have. I didn't feel that, right after his passing, I was too angry, too lost in my grief, I felt like the last four years of our lives were worthless, when they weren't, hard, yes, but never worthless.

Here's my next blog post:

Where is the man I once knew? August 6th 2016

'Today we talked about the good old days with my husband ..the days before he got sick ..and I realized that it's been a long time since I've thought about those days ..coz it's seems so long ago, it's been three years, three very long years, and there are days when it feels like forever ..you forget the days that we used to have, the really good days, when things were different..

I miss the us that we were ..I miss the husband I fell in love with, I miss the things we used to do together..

I still love my husband, but our days are shadowed by this sickness, it's all we know sometimes..

But today I realized we shouldn't forget those days, or any days for that matter. Every single day should be precious, every moment..

Some would say it's bittersweet to remember, but I don't think so ..it's powering, it makes you smile ..It's a reminder you of who you are ..When my husband is gone ..I want to remember the good days, all the things that we did together ..I don't want my only memories to be about sickness, exhaustion, pain ..I want to remember him as he was, not the way he is now.

A shell of his former self.'

I did forget, not on purpose though, but grief does funny things to your brain, it's hard to comprehend. I've only recently started remembering the good times we had, and yes sometimes they are bittersweet memories, but most are just that, memories.

Through those memories, a part of him lives on, a part of him is remembered. That is how my daughter remembers her dad, through the few memories they shared together, before he got too ill. She was after all, only three, when her dad got the diagnosis, and it did destroy something in their relationship.

My sweet little girl, had to grow up way too soon, and miss out on being just a carefree kid. But she's my kid, she's strong, and resilient, and I don't mean that in a bad way, because she knows, that sometimes, being strong, means you're strong enough to cry, strong enough to show your true emotions. She's still dealing with the loss, but she's my superstar.

I'm one of the lucky ones. I never thought I'd even want to find someone new, I was too scared of losing someone else I loved, but your heart doesn't always listen to your head, and I'm glad it didn't. Because I have an amazing new husband, he's brought so much joy into my life, and my daughter's. My little girl has an amazing new dad, to look up to. She'll never forget her real dad, she'll always have her memories and pictures, when those memories fade. I'm just glad she has someone to lean to, someone to learn from, besides myself. She's got her special daddy.

There was a time when I found it too painful to talk about, to remember, but pretty soon I realized that my daughter needed to, she needed to be able to talk about it all, and as many times as possible For a little girl, it has been extremely hard to comprehend it all. She's not stupid, she knew that her daddy was very ill, more than just a common cold, I was just too reluctant to talk to her about it, I felt like she was too young to understand, but I was wrong.

My little girl started getting migraines at the age of four, because even though we didn't tell her what was going on, doesn't mean she couldn't feel the undercurrent in every conversation. She could feel the tension in the house, she just didn't know what was causing it. I know it's a tough subject, especially to share with young kids, but people, it's so necessary, don't be brutal, but don't lie either. One good advice I got from the hospice, as cruel as it sounds, was, that after he dies, don't ever tell your child that the deceased is only sleeping, don't lie. Even small children need to grieve.

If you can’t tell your kids, then get help, get a child therapist, ask for help, for that’s why it’s there.

Chapter 5

I've talked about this before, how we need to be more vocal, to voice our feelings, our needs in the midst of all this, but sometimes, you do just need people to leave you alone, on really hard days, you wish the people would just stop, stop asking how I'm doing, how we're doing, stop being in my face, stop reminding me that we're sick. You need your own space sometimes. That's also a part of having a voice, the ability to say when you need people to leave you alone.

Will you just stop! August 6th 2016

'I love our friends, our family, but there are days, you just wish that they would stop ..stop telling us how brave, and how strong we are, stop asking how we're doing ..stop asking what you can do for us..

If and when we need something from you ..we will ask.

And for the record ..we're not brave, or strong ..we survive ..it may seem like on the outside, we're all smiles, and we may seem strong ..but you have no idea, what our reality is ..not really..

Don't try to understand or think that you know how we're feeling, coz if you're not going through what we're going through ..than you really don't know..

No offense to anyone, but what we need from you, is simply this, stand with us through this, be the shoulder we need to cry on, be the person who will lift our spirits when needed ..we don't need you to remind us that we're sick..'

Yeah, not much else to say about that. It was a really bad day, that day, and we were angry, and frustrated and a whole lot of other emotions. It was getting tougher, to keep our smiles on, to keep hoping.

Some friends are pure gold August 9th 2016

'For some time now, I've felt ..well not enough ..People around me seem to want me to be more, more than I feel I can be at the moment ..if that makes sense.. A lot of what I said in my last blog, came out of my own insecurities, my feelings of being inadequate ..I don't feel like I'm strong enough, like I have enough faith, and I know my husband feels the same. I'm not taking back what I said, nor am I apologizing, I have a right to my own feelings, and if you can't handle that, than that's not my problem, I can only be responsible for my emotions, and I refuse to take the burden of other people's feelings too. What we both need, is less drama, and more just standing with us, supporting us through this, no matter what the outcome. And some of you guys have truly understood this, and have been a really truly beautiful blessing in our lives these past months and even years. I thank God each day for sending you to our lives at a moment of absolute need.

I've come to realize (after a nudge to the right direction) that that's ok. I don't have to be more, I'm enough.

I'm releasing the guilt I've felt, though it might have been completely absurd to feel guilty in the first place, but well, I'm only human, right.

I've come to know grace, in a different kind of way, in a way like never before ..Grace to me means, I don't have to be more than I am, that I'm enough, that I'm loved regardless, that I'm precious.

Doesn't mean I'm perfect, doesn't mean I don't want to do or be better, but it means, that I'm enough as I am.

To a lot of people, faith in God means using a crutch, an excuse, or something, when bad things happen ..To me and my family, our faith is everything! You see I've never blamed God for giving us cancer, I've never blamed Him for all the bad things happening in the world, coz that's not His doing. The God I believe in ..He is my Loving Father, who's always been there for me, through the worst times during my childhood, and during the worst times in my adulthood, He is the only one, who never left me. I know some of you won't understand, and that's ok too, coz you couldn't possibly understand without knowing the real story of my life, and I know I haven't shared it to too many people, but that's because I don't trust easily, and more so it's because I don't like to feel vulnerable, completely bare, in front of people.

But that being said ..This is me, no camouflage, no pretense, take it or leave, I don't care, Because I'm ok with me.'

I've always had my faith, not religion, but faith, faith in a God that's good, so I've never been one of those to blame God for everything that's wrong with this world.

That being said, I did blame God, I blamed the world and just about everything and everyone, I needed a reason. I wanted to know why?

There has to be a higher power in play, what kind? I don't know anymore. I was raised to be a Christian, my roots are in the Salvation Army, but I don't know where my faith stands at the moment, it's not what it used to be.

Too much has happened, for me to just blindly believe that there is a good God somewhere out there. Where was the miracle we believed in? Why did he have to die and leave us? If there's a God, a good God, this shouldn't have happened, it makes no sense to me.

Even though I was raised to be a 'Christian' by values, it was never really real in our lives. My parents, while they were together, before divorcing, did go to the Salvation Army meetings, but that was because they were raised in those circles by their parents, or truthfully because my grandparents from my mother's side were from those circles. But those 'beliefs' were never really lived out in our home, so I'd say my parents were really two faced about it, and it's hard to find roots and meaning from religion or faith, if you're parents teach you that you act this way in your home but another way at church, so you had to have your church face on, no matter how bad the situation got at home. Talk about childhood drama and trauma.

I think that people who knew me before, will expect this book to be how I survived with God's help, with my faith intact, but it will be a big surprise to them, that I didn't. A lot of people do however, and I applaud them, I'm happy for them, those inspirational stories. I have one too, and a happy one, I'm just leaving God out of it.

My husband believed, to the very end, but even his faith was tested. Even with his unshakeable faith, I have never seen so much fear in anyone's eyes, than his, the moment he realized he was dying, and I don't mean months from that moment, but mere hours from that moment. He had this absolute lucid moment, three hours before he passed. Up until then, he mostly slept, didn't eat, and this was his last week in hospice.

I've told people before, that his last lucid moment was that last morning, Saturday morning, when he woke up, he was actually hungry, and asked for porridge, and ate it all, then he turned to me and asked, are you ok? And then he fell asleep again, and most people still think that that was his last moment, his last words to me, but what I'm about to tell you, is the actual truth, his final lucid moment, just mere hours before he passed away.

He had been in a deep sleep all day, people had been coming and going, saying their goodbyes, we knew the time was close, just not how close. Around eleven pm that night, I had taken a shower, while the nurses looked after my husband, and as I came back, I thought I should get some sleep, or at least try, so I went to the cot the nurses had put up for me, next to his bed, but he started to get restless all of a sudden, so I called the nurses back, and they came and upped his dosage of painkillers, at this point, he had a pain medicine pump on him, so he didn't need to swallow anything, and wait for it to kick in, that's how bad his pains had gotten.

The thing is, he wasn't awake at this point, just restless, but the nurse said to me, that if there's anyone I should call, this would be the time. I froze for a second, before doing exactly as he said, I called his parents, my dad, his uncle, and his brothers, and they all came, after I told them he wouldn't last the night.

Right before they got there, my husband woke up, he was lucid, for a brief minute, he looked at me, and asked me to pray for him. Honest to god, I have never seen such distraught, such absolute fear on anyone's eyes before, and that look has haunted me ever since. I didn't tell his parents, I couldn't. They're devout Christians, and it wouldn't have sat well with them, after that he went back to his deep sleep, and everybody arrived at the hospice.

Chapter 6

Let's go back a bit, I will readdress the subject of his last week in hospice and everything that happened after his passing.

Where am I, who am I? August 24th 2016

'A few of my friends have been asking why I haven't written anything in a while ..I guess I didn't know what to say for a while ..I've been really tired ..we've both been really tired ..I know I don't really show it much on the outside ..but the reality is ..You have to sometimes fake it to make it, I don't know how else to put it.

People always think they know me ..but the truth is, I'm scary good at hiding behind a mask ..over the years, it's just been easier that way, although lately I've tried really hard to open myself to people, the real me ..its just, that not everyone wants to see the real me, or really hear how I'm doing.

It's so much easier to be the funny, shallow person that I sometimes pretend to be ..be the clown of the group, so no one will ever take you seriously..

Which brings me to the question ..who am I? Really?

I'm actually super sensitive, and kind of serious. I do love to have fun, but on the other hand, I love my solitude,

the peace. I love to lose myself in a good book, or a good movie. I absolutely love music, I love to sing, hate performing though..

But as said ..some time's you have to fake it to make it ..especially lately ..I don't think I would've made it this far, if I hadn't faked it on times ..being sensitive makes it really hard ..because you know it doesn't take that much to make you lose it ..I don't want to fall ..I don't want to lose control ..I don't want to break..

Our week, this past week, has been harder than most weeks ..my husband's hemoglobin got way too low again, lower than in a long time ..and every time that happens, your heart stops, for just a minute, your standing on the edge again ..and yet again you have to pick up the pieces and be strong for everyone else, and for yourself..

I've noticed that my strength lies in my friends a lot ..my family ..my church ..they are my life line, my support system ..I know I should probably say my strength lies in God, and it does, but I believe that God has sent the friends we have, in to our lives right when need them the most.

There are times, as I've said before, when I feel like I want to punch my friends in the face for asking me how I'm doing too many times, but then there are the times when I need the comfort of someone asking me how I'm doing..

Yeah ..not at all sending mixed signals right ;) I know it's hard sometimes for people to be around me, and around us ..so thank you ..for being there..

So you might ask, why don't I ask help when I need it ..I do ..sometimes ..not always ..and just a word of advice, don't push me ..unless you want me to close up even more ..see this blog in it's self has been hard for me ..coz I don't open

up easily ..I don't let people see me ..I don't trust easily ..but it doesn't mean I don't want to try ..I'm learning as I go.'

I think that pretty much says it all, not much to add. I tried so desperately to hold on to what little faith I had left. I tried to pretend I didn't feel angry and disappointed and frustrated, the God I was taught to believe, wasn't answering any of our prayers. Were we talking to an empty sky? Why do people want to believe?

My pastor, at the time, said to me, please don't be one of those people who turn bitter after a loss. What a weird thing to say. I couldn't have possibly have known how I would react afterwards, so how could I promise anyone anything?

Pastors, aren't always the easiest people to get along with, especially in our situation. They can be almost bullies, because they want a certain outcome, they want us to keep our faith, they want us to trust them and God blindly, never waver. Because when we fail in our faith, they abandon us, when we fail in the expectations they have for us, they abandon us. You have to be good enough, to be enough.

I know they're only human, and humans fail, more times than not, but it doesn't mean I have to keep people like that in my life. After everything, I needed space, I needed to unplug for a while. People didn't like that, so they broke all ties to me. Obviously it's a longer story then that, but I'll get to it later.

It's hardest on the kids August 27th 2016

'I think it's always hardest on the kids to go through this ..it leaves a permanent mark, that they are not yet ready to face, or don't completely understand.

We have a six year old daughter, and I also have a 17 year old step-son, and it's been hard, watching them go through this, because they are so far apart in age, they also react very differently.

Mostly I'm worried about our six year old, just because she lives with us, she sees this disease all day long, all week, all month long, all year long ..She was only three years old, when her daddy was diagnosed, so half of her life, daddy has been sick.

One of the conversations we had today in the car, when I got off from work, was something like this;

Jo; Daddy are you going to be sick forever, it's like you've been sick a thousand years already. You are really sick aren't you, it's bad?

Dad; Yeah, I'm sick, until God heals me.

Jo; Right, He will heal you in heaven.

(this would've been a good point to have the death talk, and say yeah, in heaven, which probably would have led to the question, when is daddy going to heaven and so on, but I so wasn't ready for anything like that, so...)

Dad; Yes in heaven, but God can heal me here too, on earth, I don't have to go to heaven to be healed.

We got home at that point, so the subject was dropped and we didn't revisit it. Not today.

On one hand, I believe in miracles, and we, and a lot of other people have been praying for a miracle, for a long time ..but nothing has happened yet, and we are really disappointed, not at God, but just because we haven't received our miracle yet.

But on one hand, I'm pretty realistic, so I would want to be prepared too, just in case, and to me, that isn't like I don't

trust or believe in God, no nothing like that. But to me, the miracle we're waiting and my faith, aren't connected, what I mean is, if my husband dies, it won't change my faith, although, I'll be asking God some questions when I get to heaven..

The fact is, we don't always get the answers we're looking for, not until we meet God face to face, but that shouldn't change our faith. The Bible says that we believe in the things we don't yet see. We can't see heaven, or God, but it doesn't change the fact that we keep believing in them.

Our faith, should be based on trust, always. I trust that even though I don't see everything, and I don't know everything, and things don't always go my way, that God still has my back, He will carry me through the storms of life.

I don't know, why my husband hasn't been healed yet, but I trust, that God knows, and no matter what the outcome of this is, He will carry us through.'

There's so much faith in this one blog post, the desperate need to cling to that final hope. I wanted to have so much faith, faith like my husband did, and yet, when he died, that last night, that utter terror I saw in his eyes, made me wonder what was on the other side, and if my faith had been misplaced all these years. I did get bitter, and angry after he died, I couldn't fathom, why God, who is supposed to be good, could allow him to die in such a horrific way. That's not a God I want to know, that's a dictator, who does what he wills when he wills it, a proper god complex, being all high and mighty, and not giving a damn about the people he supposedly created.

I tried so hard, to cling to the shattered pieces of my faith. I think it's normal, when you're facing death, that you desperately need to believe in something higher, that there's an afterlife, that your loved one didn't just simply cease to exist. Makes their passing easier. Whether there is such a place, only time will tell.

Chapter 7

What happens to us as we grow older? September 3th 2016

'You know, when I was younger, a lot younger, I wanted to be a doctor when I grew up, and a singer, and a writer ;)

But as we grow older, everything changes ..we change ..but why..? What happens to our dreams ..what happens to us to make us forget that we ever had them, and is it too late to reach for them now?

I truly hope, I never do or say anything to my daughter to make her believe that she can't reach for the stars if that is what she wants. I want to be an inspiration. To her, and hopefully to others as well.

For years I've known where my passions lie, but I haven't done anything about them ..for so long I felt dead inside ..only recently I've felt like I'm coming out of my shell again ..I feel ..like me again ..I feel alive..

My daughter has a gift ..a true gift from God ..the gift of supernatural love ..she loves people, it's as simple as that ..and I hope she never loses it.

It's never too late to dream...and chase after your dreams..

I hope that I can stand next to, and support the people around me, to encourage them to believe in dreams ..and

always have faith. To always believe that you are worthy ..because you truly are.'

Well, yeah I think that post speaks for its self. Sometimes becoming a grown up makes you think, that your dreams are over, or at least a bit more realistic, you've got a home to look after, you've got bills to pay you've got to work non-stop to pay for those bills, and in the process, we tend to forget what really matters.

My husband worked up until two months before he died, because he was scared how we would ever manage financially otherwise, and because it was a distraction, he didn't have to think about being sick when he was working, he even got promoted right before he died.

All that money, all the effort, all the time he spent away from his family, he can't have it back and he couldn't take any of it with him. Why do we waste time? I understand that in this economy you have to work in order to provide even food for your family and a roof over their heads, but let's not forget, that when you are with your family and loved ones, that you unplug from all that. Enjoy every single minute you have with them, because you will never have that time back.

This sucks so bad! September 4th 2016

'This weeks just been...bad...to say the least..

Like I've said before, there are good days, and bad days and then there's those in between ..lately there's just been too many bad days in a row ..and we are so tired..

and it shows ..I can't really truly focus on anything, I seem to be drifting ..not really present ..it's hard to explain..

I hate this! I don't know what else to say today, but I hate this! Why do we need to suffer, why does my husband need to suffer so much, what's the point?!

It rips your heart apart, every time you see the pain on your husbands face, when you see the endless tears, and hear the sounds of agony, and there is absolutely nothing I can do to help ..so what's the point..?

I don't have the strength today ..I just don't..

As I write this, I try to focus on music, just soak up the presence of worship, to feel God's arms around me and mine ..and let me tell you, it's not easy, but as you surrender everything, and there is no more fight left in you, that's when He makes His presence known. I think that's the key a lot of times, when things are bad, and you don't know what to do, or how to fight any longer, you give it up, you surrender, you stop fighting in your own strength, and just let God fight the battle for you. In the end it comes back to the same truth I wrote about before; Trust.

There is this one song I've listened to, over and over, song by Lauren Daigle, called: Trust in You (you can find it on YouTube).

This one was hard to read back, I had so much faith before, and yet I didn't. The song I used to listen, I can't do that anymore, it sort of pisses me off, listening to it now. The underlying feelings, I never shared them, I wanted people around us to think we were holding on, that our faith was unshaken, that I was the person I had portrayed to be all these years. This meek girl, who silently followed in her husband's footsteps, doing exactly what everybody else was expecting me to do and be.

Who I am, is only now starting to come out, because I'm surrounded by people who would accept me in any way I was. I get to choose, as funny as that sounds, at the age of 32, I can finally, truly choose for myself, what and who I believe in, all of it. There's no one dictating how I'm supposed to live my life or what I'm supposed to believe in.

I'm free to be me. I was silent for so many years, due to my upbringing and then marrying so young the first time, I was only 19, in case you didn't do the math before. I was still in the process of finding who I was, but instead I allowed someone stronger, more independent person to show me and teach me how he thought I should be. I'm not saying this as a bitter woman, don't get me wrong. I chose my life back then, just as I'm choosing my life now, the difference is, I know who I am now, and I'm strong enough to stand my ground.

I don't in all honesty, know if I can ever get back my faith, the way it was before, I don't know if I want to. There are obviously still so many unresolved feelings inside me, that needs to be resolved. In my blog, I talk, and I go back to my faith and God a lot of times, but that's because I had nothing else to hold onto. It was the one thing I was told was the only right thing to do. Furthermore, when you're in situation like that, you kind of need that reassurance that there's something else out there, that there's a better place for those that pass. It gives you a sense of peace and reassurance, to think, that your loved ones are safe, there's no more pain and suffering. But faith is blind, and at this moment in my life, I can't do blindness, I need to see where I'm going.

We had so many plans for our lives. My life would look very different, had he survived the cancer. We would have more kids together, we would attend the church he chose for us, I would be a youth leader in that church, and our lives would be the absolute opposite to the life I'm living now.

But I broke down, completely broke into pieces after he died, and I couldn't pick up the pieces up again, I had to rebuild me, from the scratch, and in that process I learned so much about myself, I didn't know before, the woman I was and was going to be, was gone, completely gone, and in its place emerged this strong wilful beautiful woman, a woman who had to turn into a warrior to save her family from sinking to the abyss.

This woman is independent, and resolved to build her daughter up the same way. I want her to become everything that she could ever dream of becoming and more. I want her to be able to trust herself in every situation, in every choice that she makes, and I know she will, because she's got my support and her new dad's support all the way, no matter what.

This next blog post is from October 2016, a day in our lives, or well a week of our lives, and this was every week.

'Well I don't really talk about what our days and weeks look like normally, so here goes nothing.

Our normal routine at the moment;

Monday: Blood tests

Tuesday: A few bags of blood

Wednesday: More blood transfusions

Thursday: kind of normal (finally)

Friday: Normal I guess

Saturday: Already feeling the loss of blood, low hemoglobin

Sunday: Really tired, really low hemoglobin

All in all, lots of sleeping, maybe going to work on 1-3 days a week, depending how he is feeling..

Lots of medication ..I mean a lot, there is a whole box with just his meds, and then some. This is our every weekly routine, well then there are worse weeks, and different things happening on those occasions. Like this week, we had a meeting today with the palliative care for cancer patients ..that was hard ..emotionally, and then on Sunday, after church, we are meeting with the doctor from a hospice facility ..not going to be easy either..

Yup ..that's about it, in a nutshell

Welcome to our world of cancer.

In those things in mind. I'm trying to work full-time, I'm starting translations in our church this Sunday, I'm also part of our youth team, and I'm doing other stuff too ..well trying to ..it's a juggle..'

Obviously that's not all that happened on our week to week basis, but close enough. I was trying to be very busy, because it was too hard for me to be home, too hard to see him suffer endlessly, so I joined in on the youth work of our church and also helped to translate to people who didn't speak English, since our church was bilingual, if that's the right word. I did whatever shifts at work, I was a workaholic.

It was just too hard at that point. His breathing was getting worse, because he was losing so much weight that he didn't have the muscles to breathe normally anymore, so I avoided going into the bedroom, because listening to him trying and struggling to breathe was so hard, we also had a special mattress on his side of the bed to prevent bedsores, and a chair for shower, because he was too tired to stand under the shower by himself.

You can't even imagine, how hard that was to watch, a proud strong young man, and now he was falling apart in front of me. It was even harder for him, his self-image really suffered from it all, and it was bad at times.

It's not a life I would want on anyone. You know you would expect to see those things when you're talking about very old people that are near death, not when you're talking about a 37-year-old man. It's hard to imagine, until you're there, in that very situation.

Chapter 8

This next blog post is from November, barely a month before he passed away.

It takes a lot, not giving anything back November 7th 2016

'It's been a while again ..since my last entry ..I just don't know what to say ..my life is falling apart, and me along with it ..I thought, that after all this time, I would barely feel a thing ..I've kept telling myself, that if I just distance myself from all of it, from him, that I would spare myself from all the pain that's coming ..I was lying to myself ..it hurts ..so bad ..you can hardly breathe..

For over ten years we've been together ..that's a long time ..but recently I've come to notice that it's not long enough ..it's not..

I've tried to distract myself from reality ..by books, by movies, by hours spent on the computer, and by even using people ..doesn't work..

I'm so ready to leave all this behind me...and at the same time, I'm not ..I don't know who I am without him..

I just want the suffering to end ..It breaks your heart every time to see him suffer ..piece by piece, until I'm scared

there'll be nothing left to break ..How much of me will there be left..?

I feel so lost, so confused, so scared ..I never want to love again ..I never want to feel this pain again...All I ever wanted out of life, was to be happy..

I'm not asking your opinion, or your permission to feel whatever I feel, let's make that clear, since it seems to come up a lot, especially behind my back. I have every right to feel whatever I feel, every right to react however I do. My reactions are my own, the way I handle things, are my ways. I don't give a damn if you approve my methods.

You might not agree with me, or my methods, but I don't care. This is my life! You don't have to understand me or anything I do or say or feel..

Now that that's out in the open ..let's continue ..shall we..

People that have never had to deal with a dying loved one, will never understand most of the things that we go through ..You don't understand the process that comes with it ..the hope, the denial, the anger, and finally the acceptance of things ..In case of someone who has been sick a long time ..the grieving process feels endless, because you start grieving, long before that person is dead ..you have to mentally prepare yourself to what's to come ..and it's so hard ..you have no idea..

I've also been criticized for still working, instead of staying home with my dying husband ..You know, let me ask you this ..In what world do you live in?! What is wrong with you?? My sanity depends on the fact, I can get out of the house every now and then ..When it matters, in the end, of course I will be by my husband's side, and I'm by his side, even now, whether I'm actually home, doesn't matter, because we are in this together! So since a lot of you have asked me, what can you say or do when you hear my story, here is an advice on what NOT to do or say.

I still have to provide for my family, I still have to buy food, and pay bills. I still have to continue my life, even when I don't feel like it.

Ok, enough of that ..I'm so tired of being angry with stupid people ..so stop being stupid ..show some compassion, and understanding, and love ..be there in a way that matters, or lose my friendship..

There are times, I wish you guys would just leave me alone ..and there are times I need you more than anything ..so go figure what do I really need.. A really good advice would be, to listen, when I tell you what I, and we need, even if you have to ask the same question a thousand times, make the effort, and I will value it..

I know I'm not the easiest person to get along with ..so thank you, for those, who have stick it with me all this time.

I wish that our story could have been different ..I wish that we would've handled everything differently ..I so wanted to have the kind of blog joey and Rory had(thislifeilive.com) filled with love, and warmth, and hope and faith ..even though joey died, the blog was amazing, and still is, in so many ways ..the way Rory wrote it, even though it was super hard on them, you could read the love that was in every entry..

Our story ..hasn't been like that ..our faith hasn't been that strong ..our love has been tested in so many ways ..our story ..isn't beautiful..

I don't know what life has in store for us in the future ..I don't want to know ..I'm just trying really hard to survive from one day to the next..'

Ok, wow, I didn't even remember writing this one, or some of the other entries as well. I think it's because I wrote my blog in the moment. It's based on my feelings, my every day struggles. It's real. I do apologize for jumping from one thing to the next and then going back to something that I already wrote about, but you see, this isn't about me writing everything in perfect order, or even perfectly, this is about going through my story, my years with this illness, and my years with my husband, and sometimes that requires a little mess, in the end I hope you can see the picture I'm trying to paint with my words.

In this particular entry, you can definitely see me already falling apart, my world as I knew it, crumpling into pieces, my faith tested in ways I didn't know about. The brokenness was so visible, tangible. It's hard to read about the fears and hurt I was going through, knowing now, what was still coming, and knowing that there was nothing to prepare me for it. I tried watching videos about cancer, reading articles, just learning anything and everything I could about it, and yet, nothing prepared me for it in the end.

One of the reasons, why I'm keeping this book as it is, messy, and raw and sometimes all over the place, is because it's the best way for me to really show you what life is like, really like, when you're living with this. It's messy, emotional and raw and all over the place, and I'm not going to make it pretty for you, just to make it easier on you. This is the book you've chose to read, and knowing the topic, you probably knew it would be hard to read, emotionally and all, so hang tight, and I hope to show you in the end, that there's life afterwards, even when you don't see it immediately.

And here we go November 20th 2016

'Well, this upcoming week will be different, and new..

My husband is going to a hospice hospital on Monday, he is going there by an ambulance ride, since he can't drive anymore ..his pain management is all over the place, so he is going in, to get it back to balance, and then he can come back home ..the stressful part in this, is the fact we don't know if it's going to take two days, or a week or more before he comes back, and I have to figure out how to do my work and be able to look after my daughter, you know, pick her up, and taking her every morning to daycare ..I guess it's really time to use every offer of help we can get..

Well, I just have to remember, that we need to do this, in order for my husband to feel better ..and it's just a start ..since we both know that there will come a day, when he will fully enter hospice, and at that time ..we know he isn't coming back ..so this is just a beginning ..he will from now on, be coming and going to the hospice place ..and they will keep visiting us every week..

I'm just desperately trying to wrap my head around all of this ..I've known a long time, where this is heading ..but to really start preparing for it ..in our everyday lives...it's gruesome..

How will I survive with my daughter all alone?

I know that I have family and friends, that will do the best they can to help ..but at the end of the day ..it'll just be me and Jo..

What will our lives look like..?

How much is this going to affect my daughter's life..? How will she survive..?'

This entry I posted in the end of November, it was the very first time he ever went voluntarily to the hospice, and he went there to get better pain meds, but he also went there to give him time to rest, and to give us, me and my daughter, a few days to rest as well. It may sound cruel and selfish, but we all needed it, that small breather. In the beginning, I had said to my husband that, there's no way he's going into hospice if that time ever becomes a reality, I'm your wife, and I will look after you at home, it's my responsibility. He said to me then, which I didn't agree at the time, that I had no idea what I was promising, I had no idea how bad he would get, and that he would never put that burden on me. Looking back now, I see the wisdom in it, I never could've been able to look after him, the way the hospice did, they were a lifesaver.

However, he didn't spend that much time there, the hospice nurses came to our house twice or three times a week in the end, so he was able to stay home almost until the end.

Small moments December 6th 2016

'It's been almost four years ..since this chapter in our lives started ..and my god it's been a rollercoaster...the good, the bad and everything in between..

I'm not the same person I was four years ago ..I've had to learn to be stronger, to show mercy, to myself ..to forgive myself, and accept that this is the way I cope with things..

I don't want to go back ..to the way I was ..I am stronger as a person because of this ..and I won't apologize for it..

Does it makes things easier ..no ..I'm at a breaking point ..falling apart ..desperately trying to hide how broken I am..

Everyday it get's harder and harder ..to be near my husband ..as he is now...kills me ..don't get me wrong, I do love him, but the man I fell in love with...is long gone ..he is nothing but a shell of a former life..

To accept ..that our lives will never go back to the way it was ..breaks my heart..

But there are small moments ..moments of peace, moments of joy and laughter, moments of oblivion, moments when you can forget ..for just a moment..

I won't apologize for anything ..anything that I do to make me feel better, however I decide to cope ..how I make myself forget ..just for a moment..

We all have our own methods of survival ..I would never judge anyone for doing whatever they needed to do ..reality will hit eventually, let's show some mercy to ourselves ..and allow the small moments of oblivion..

I'm not sure what the future holds ..or if I'm even ready to face it ..there's so much pain in me right now ..the weight of it all is crushing me ..I'm not ready to be alone..

I need to show my daughter that we can get through this ..so I'll do whatever it takes to survive.'

The last month of our lives was upon us, and we didn't even know it. Who am I kidding, of course we knew, we just refused to believe it, we pretended that it wasn't happening, but we knew, deep down. At this point of time, he was tired and sleeping all the time, barely staying awake an hour at a time. He was thin, skin and bone, he really looked so fragile, you had to wonder how he was even standing.

Chapter 9

Time is running out December 13th 2016

'I thought we had more time ..but time is not on our side ..and life isn't fair ..to anyone

It's two more weeks before Christmas ..but our time ..is focused on spending it with my husband ..because he might not last long after that ..it's time ..to say our goodbyes ..it doesn't matter if we are ready...we weren't given a chance..

I had to tell my six year old daughter that her daddy's not coming home for Christmas ..that he's not coming home at all..

How do you tell a child that it's
her daddy's last weeks..

I thought about not posting this ..out of respect towards my husband ..he doesn't need the extra attention ..what we need right now ..is to be left alone ..to spent whatever time we have left ..together in peace ..as a family

I'm not saying you can't say your goodbyes if you feel like it ..but be respectful..'

It was indeed time to say goodbye, however, my daughter never did get that chance. We had it scheduled that he would go to the hospice on Wednesday a week and a half before

Christmas, to stay indefinitely, we didn't set a time, but we knew, however, that he wasn't coming back. But things took a turn for the worse that weekend, and two am that Saturday, I had to call the ambulance to come pick him up and take him to the hospice a few days earlier than planned.

He got a pain pump at the hospice, to help him with the immense pain he was in, I stayed with him as much as I could, I took and pick up my daughter from day-care but other than that, I was always there, my dad was my angel at that time, and he helped with my daughter as well, and tried to stay with my husband as often as possible. The first time I really got out of the hospital, was that last Saturday, when his brother came to take me out to lunch and get a change of clothes from home before going back. People came and went, to say their goodbyes, my husband, he slept more and more, was barely awake a few hours a day. That last weekend, I remember it like yesterday. My friend came by to pick up my daughter, so she could spend some time with their three daughters and I could spend some time alone with my husband, little did I know, how little time I had left.

We had planned to bring Christmas to him, to the hospice, but we never had the chance. This is my next blog post.

It's Christmas, and he's gone December 24th 2016

'In my last entry, I said it was time to say goodbye ..at that time, I thought we had more time, at least until Christmas ..but God had other plans, and my husband was too tired to wait until then ..as most of you know ..my husband passed away, 2 am, on the 18th of December ..a mere week before Christmas ..and my daughter and I ..we're

left to pick up the pieces ..of a life that seems so empty now that he's gone..

I'm not brave ..I'm not strong ..I'm a wreck ..I'm lost ..my heart is in thousand pieces ..I lost my best friend ..the love of my life ..and there's no going back on that..

I may look strong on the outside ..but on the inside ..I'm breaking apart ..but I can't afford to lose it ..I have a daughter to think of ..she needs to know that it's ok to cry and miss daddy, but she also needs to know, that we're going to be ok ..that's what I need to convey to her by my actions ..I don't try to hide my feelings from her ..I'm only trying to teach her ..that life has to continue..

Do I really feel that way ..my god no ..absolutely not ..but I'm trying ..I'm smiling ..even when I feel like crying ..I keep telling her and myself in the process, that we're going to be ok, just the two of us ..and yet I'm so scared..

I'm glad though ..that there was so much family present during his final hours ..I can't thank you guys enough for what it meant to me ..I couldn't have done it alone..

I just ..I'm still waiting ..for him to come home ..it hasn't completely sunk in ..that he's really gone ..I sat with him ..after he died ..for two and a half hours ..looking at his chest ..thinking that any minute now ..I'll see him breathing again ..leaving him there...was the hardest thing I've ever done ..I just ..I left him..

I know he's in a better place, he's finally home in heaven, there's no more pain ..it's what he wanted ..he was so tired ..he just wanted to go home ..and so I sat with him that night, praying with him, coz he asked me to ..and telling him it was ok ..it was ok to go ..that we would be ok ..and I held his hand, stroked his hair and just sat there ..until he

took his last breathe ..last breathe on earth ..first breathe in heaven ..he was finally home, after a long battle..

Our hearts are broken right now ..but we have a healer in heaven ..and one day ..we'll be ok ..one day ..I'll see him again ..I trust in that..

Merry Christmas to my love in heaven ..I'll be thinking of you..'

I never thought I'd say this, but it does get easier, I know it doesn't feel like it will, it will take time, but you will, eventually, find your footing again in this world. I went through this manic phase, where I didn't stop, Jo had to go back to day-care, I had to go back to work, and man did I work my butt off, I couldn't stop, I felt like if I did, I'd never start again, I'd never get up again.

However, I had to. My dad was basically taking care of my daughter while I was working non-stop, but he was grieving too, and I had to give him some space to do that. So I decided that I would take a year off from work, spent some time with my daughter, and help her adjust to life in school and life in general. But as many of you know, there has to come a time, when you stop, you fall, and you break down, and that's what happened to me. Once I gave myself permission to stop and really feel, it was hard, it was so hard, it took a lot of crying, a lot of sleepless nights and very little food, but my fear of not being able to get up again, didn't luckily come true.

We are still here and life has to move on January 4th 2017

'To be honest, I thought I was done writing ..since this blog was about us as a family going through cancer and everything that came with it..

Well everything I wrote about, all the fears, all of it ..it came true ..I talked a lot before about us having a death sentence, him dying and all that ..but you see ..the way my husband lived this time, made me believe, that he was going to make it, or maybe I just wanted so badly to hold on to that dream..

I was there ..in hospice ..for the last week ..now thinking back to that time ..it doesn't seem real ..it was like a nightmare ..a nightmare I couldn't wake up from ..every minute was like a eternity ..mostly what I did, was sit beside his bed, held his hand, stroked his hair, talked to him ..I tried so hard to seem happy, and ok, and I even told him I was ok, so that he wouldn't worry ..but of course I wasn't ..I was terrified..

I couldn't comprehend the situation ..I was right there, next to him ..but I felt like I wasn't there, but that I was somewhere deep inside me ..trying to shelter me, trying to keep it together..

Every passing day took more of him away from me ..I watched him disappear..

I was lucky to have my dad there the whole week ..but I know it wasn't easy on him either, he loved my husband, so it felt like losing a son in a way ..we did a lot of crying together during that week..

I'll never forget the moment...when he took his last breathe ..his family surrounding him ..all the love in the room ..it didn't make it any easier ..but I'm so thankful they were there ..I never would've made it through the night without them..

The moment he died...I just...I had to walk out for a moment ..I just ..I couldn't breathe ..I could barely stand ..so I sat on one of the sofas outside the room ..and just completely fell apart ..you see ..during these years when he was sick ..I never allowed myself to fall apart ..not really...but then ..my god ..all the pain inside me from years of not crying ..just came out..

I probably woke up everyone with my crying ..but I couldn't stop ..I just wanted to scream ..until I had no voice left ..and my superhero dad was there, he came out of the room, and just held me ..he was crying as hard as me ..but he wouldn't let go ..he held on ..until I could breathe again..

I felt empty ..so lost ..afterwards ..but I managed to say goodbye to his family and only my dad and I stayed behind ..I have to say my dad is my superhero, for being there ..I know he was exhausted ..but he never left my side ..so we sat there for two and a half hours ..just watching him ..the hardest thing I ever did was leaving him behind when we finally left at 04.30 in the morning..

But life does move on ..as much pain as we've been through in all of this ..we are still here, we're alive ..and I'm finally starting to remember the good times, the times we had together before he got sick, and those are the things I want to remember ..not the night he died ..but the man that lived.

There's finally peace in our house, it's finished, and we can breathe again ..there are times when we cry and miss him ..but there are more and more times when we smile and laugh..

I don't want to forget him, and I won't, he was such a huge part of my life, he made me into the person I am, he was my best friend..

But I finally feel...happy ..more me ..the weight is gone from my shoulders ..now I just need to figure out who we are without him ..and I will ..in time..

there's still the last chapter in all of this ..and it's coming ..the funeral ..once we get through that, I believe we can finally start to heal ..it's the last goodbye to an amazing man he was..

And he was ..amazing ..and that's the memory I want to stick to ..and that is what I'll teach my daughter...to remember her daddy as the amazing dad that he was..

But our lives will move on, and we'll be happy again ..we'll love again ..we'll be whole again ..a whole family..

Our lives will be different ..but only that, it's not worse than before, just different ..but we have people in our lives that love us, that'll get us through the worse periods..

I'm ready to look to the future again ..I'm ready to be happy again ..and I'm ready to open my heart again ..and that's something ..coz I thought that I would never do that ..that I was safer behind my walls ..the fear of losing someone else I love ..is very real right now ..and feeling anything feels scary ..I think that that fear will be with me for some time ..It's just ..when you've been through what I've been through ..you really don't ever want to go through that again ..but what I've realized lately is that by choosing not to love again ..you lose ..it may save you from a lot of heartache ..but that's not living ..it's hiding ..and I don't want to hide

My life may have been insane at times, crazy, and painful ..but I wouldn't change a thing ..coz if I did...if I had chosen not to love my husband ..I never would've had all the happy memories I have now, the memories that will carry us through ..I would've saved us from a lot of hurt ..but just look at the life that we did have together ..he was a blessing to our lives..

It's time ..to start anew ..life has to move on ..and I'm ready ..I'm not scared anymore ..I know I'm not alone.'

I'm here today, as a living proof, that you can get through even the most horrific things, you might not feel like you can, but you can. It will change you, there's no way through something like this, without it changing you profoundly. I went through hell, to find who I am and where I belong.

Two years and three months later, I'm living in England with my husband, my precious second husband. He is my light and my love, my support. He's a brilliant dad and role model for my little girl. I never thought I'd find love again, but I'm so blessed that I did.

Along the way I lost a lot of people from our lives. People didn't agree with the way I handled things after his death, they said a lot of hurtful things about me. Most never talked to me again. I was told I shouldn't date anyone for at least two years, that I should morn him respectfully and reflect on who I am alone before I can be with someone. It's bullshit, I've never told anyone how or how long they should grieve someone, and I'm not going to do that now either. We are all individuals, our own kind of persons, and everybody grieves differently. I lost my husband long before he died, this illness took him away from me long before then. I grieved every single day he was alive, and when he died, it killed something in me. I'm lucky, so lucky and blessed, that I was able to find love again, I know that for some people, that never happens, and that's ok too.

I'm going to leave you with this last blog post, which, I'll admit was an angry one, but it does convey my true feelings. Don't ever give up hope, you will rise again from the ashes, you're a Warrior.

Cancer freaking sucks but life doesn't February 8th 2017

'That's what I wrote in the top of the page when I first started writing this blog ..Not because I felt it, or believed it, but because I desperately wanted to believe it.

Cancer sucks, but life doesn't ..but our lives did ..suck ..big time ..and I know it's not what people want to hear ..it never is ..what people want ..is to hear stories that build them up, that inspire them, that gives them courage and strength, and faith for a better tomorrow..

But life's not a fairytale ..and since I've been criticized about pretty much anything and everything, I might as well piss more people by writing the truth ..the real truth ..behind the beautifully molded words and sentences that I used before in my writing..

Before, when I was writing here I tried being honest but not brutally so ..I wanted to give people a glimpse of what our lives were like, but I knew that most people, they wouldn't or couldn't be able to handle the reality, the real brutal reality, that we lived in..

Do you really think, that love solves everything, or that faith solves everything, coz it doesn't, it's great if you have

them both, but at the end of the day, you're only human ..fragile, broken..

I didn't ask for this life ..I didn't ask for the pain we went through ..No one ever does, and no one, absolutely no one deserves to have cancer ..but cancer doesn't choose from only good or only from bad ppl..no.it doesn't give you a choice ..it fucking sucks..

I hated It ..hated everything about it ..it destroyed our lives, it ruined everything I ever held dear ..the man I fell in love it, died long before cancer even took him ..there was nothing left..

People have a very bad habit of putting other people on a pedestal, after they pass away ..they become heroes, or icons, examples..

But it's not true ..the real heroes ..are those left behind ..like my little girl ..she survived ..she continues her story ..she continues her life ..we both do ..she is my hero

There is no such thing as a perfect person ..we're all broken ..one way or another..

I have to wonder ..why is it so easy to judge other people?? How much does it take ..what has to happen, before people really see what they're doing to other's ..stop being cruel ..stop judging ..stop thinking that you're somehow better than others ..at the end, before God ..we are all judged the same way..

I've always tried to be honest, visible, so that people can see through me ..but over the years, I've noticed that people will use that against you, they will hurt, intentionally or otherwise ..so since early on ..I've learned to build up walls ..to protect myself ..to make myself hard on the outside ..so nothing can touch you ..you also build up defenses ..like hurting people first, before they have a chance of hurting you ..you run ..and you don't look back..

It doesn't matter if you're 13..or 30..it hurts just as much ..why does it hurt..?? Because you care ..because in spite of all the walls you've built, you open your heart to care ..and end up getting hurt..

To those reading this ..I don't need to tell you which ones ..I'm sure you will feel it in you're heart ..or not ..I actually don't care ..but let me tell you this ..for so long I was angry, pist off would describe it better ..but I want to tell you I forgive you ..intentional or unintentional ..it doesn't matter ..you hurt me ..and I don't want you in my life anymore ..I forgive you, so I can move on, but I don't need you in my life anymore ..That's the great part in all this ..I get to choose my friends..

There's a difference between honesty and just simply being mean, cruel ..harsh ..I do understand that many of you are still grieving, and that my post hurt your feelings ..and I'm sorry for that, but I'm not responsible for your feelings, only mine..

I'm not ashamed to tell the world I'm finally happy

Grief is different for each person ..do not judge me, according to your own standards, thinking that you know better, that you know me better, or that you have some right in telling me, an adult, how to live my life

I will stir a lot of conversation, a lot of judgment no doubt, but to be honest, I don't care anymore ..it's this thing called freedom of speech ..I don't need your permission, and I don't need you to like my post ..if you read it, it's your choice ..but don't come crying to me how I've hurt you're feelings again ..leave me alone, once and for all..

That is the honest truth ..the ugly truth ..deal with it..

I'm proud of myself, proud that I was able to trust again, with my heart ..proud that I was able to love again, after everything I've been through ..I know that I deserve to be happy ..and I know that my husband would be happy for me ..he hated seeing me so sad ..broken ..he knew, first hand ..what his cancer did to our family ..he saw how it broke us apart..

My husbands memory will never fade ..he will be with us for the rest of our lives ..but our lives will move on ..it has to ..we can't stop living ..I'm still dealing with things, which is natural ..and I'm sure I will go through a lot over the years to come ..but I wont stop living because of it..

If you want to barricade yourselves behind closed doors for months ..that's your choice ..and I would never ever judge you for it ..so don't judge me for dealing with things my own way ..there's no right or wrong way to deal with grief ..there's only your way..

I mourned my husband for a long time ..long before he died...in a way I was alone for a long time ..but you could never understand that ..not unless you've been through what I've been through ..I know that a lot of you, couldn't accept the fact he was dying ..but we knew ..for over a year, we knew that he was dying ..we had to deal with it for a long time..

I guess, most of you didn't know that ..why? Because we knew, both of us knew, that a lot of you, could never accept that ..So we smiled, and nodded to everything you said ..we let you in, into our homes, into our lives, we let you stay in the belief that we were stronger than we were ..why?

Because it's what you needed ..but in silence ..we knew ..and it hurt..

We loved all the prayers, we truly did, and all the positive and encouraging thoughts you sent our way ..but in silence ..we knew ..and it hurt..

Like I said, people don't want to hear that ..they want to see strong people, they want to be encouraged ..they want...they need ..what we needed ..truly ..were people, who would just stand with us through all this ..but very few did ..and I love you for it ..it takes a lot of strength to be there, in that situation ..we didn't need you to try to solve things, we didn't need your advice, all we needed, was for you to be there

We only get one life ..let's live it to the fullest ..don't be afraid to love again ..I'm not.'

You might say, well, didn't you feel like you didn't have the right to feel relieved and happy after he was gone? Well let me tell you, I did, for a long time after he was gone, I felt like I was cheating on him, like I was betraying him. Like I wasn't supposed to be happy again. I went through so many different emotions, so many stages of grief that I didn't know existed.

Let me try to explain this. My first husband said to me, that he would rather be dead, then sick and in pain all the time, that it would be a relief, and I have to say, he was right. It's not a cruel thing to say, but just honest. I never in my life thought that euthanasia was right, I thought it was horrible, and I still can't really wrap my head around it, but my point is, during those years when he was sick, the idea of him finally being free of all the pain, was an idea that brought peace in the end. As much as it hurt, to say goodbye and let go, I was relieved that he was finally at peace, no more pain, no more sorrow for him.

Life is too short, to live with regrets. Live it to the fullest. Be happy, every second of your life counts. Your feelings matter too. Don't let people put you down. Be honest to yourself, let yourself feel, and then let it go, and move on. There are more adventures waiting to happen.